FAMILY

THE
BRIDEGROOM'S
HANDBOOK

SEAN CALLERY

WARD LOCK

A WARD LOCK BOOK

First published in the UK
1992 by Ward Lock
(a Cassell imprint)
Villiers House
41/47 Strand
London
WC2N 5JE

Distributed in Australia
by Capricorn Link (Australia) Pty Ltd
P.O. Box 665, Lane Cove, NSW 2066

British Library Cataloguing-in-Publication Data

A catalogue record for this book is available from the British Library

ISBN 0–7063–7070–8

Typeset in 11 on 11½ point ITC Garamond Light by
Columns Design and Production Services Ltd, Reading

Cover photograph: Nick Carter-Pegg

Printed and bound in Great Britain by
HarperCollins, Glasgow

CONTENTS

INTRODUCTION

When people are discussing weddings, they talk about the day as being the happiest in the bride's life. The bridegroom hardly gets a look-in. 'All you have to do,' he is told, 'is turn up on time.'

Such advice disregards a number of other things the groom must do, and places him in a secondary role which does not fit the reality of many weddings today. Just as marriage is a partnership, so is arranging the wedding, and the days when all the arrangements (and the bills) were left to the bride's family are over. Many couples live together (or virtually do so) before they are married, and many also make a considerable financial contribution to the wedding. Their greater intimacy prior to marriage forms a closer bond which allows them to take a much more central role in organizing the event.

As these trends have developed, so the role of the bridegroom has changed. Men today can choose to be totally involved in every aspect of the wedding. This helps to make the big day itself a celebration of the partnership of marriage, instead of just a great send-off for the bride.

Engaged couples today face a large number of choices about where to marry (church or registry office?), what kind of reception to have (grand sit-down meal, informal buffet, at an hotel, in a marquee?) and whether to have an evening party too (disco for friends and those you were unable to invite to the service, a quiet dinner with your relations) or a meal with your new spouse to commence your honeymoon. Choosing requires making a decision on the kind of wedding you want, and much sifting of information of the options available.

There are plenty of books giving advice on how to be the best man, but very few for the bridegroom. Yet the wedding would always be able to go ahead in the absence of the best man, but it would come to a halt pretty fast if the husband-to-be were off the scene! Indeed, in many ways the balance of responsibility and involvement has shifted from the best man to the bridegroom over the last few years: few best men carry out all the tasks traditionally allocated to them, and many of these duties are taken over by the bridegroom.

Weddings have retained their significance as one of the major rituals in our lives. One of the myths which has been maintained about them is that the day is all about the bride. It isn't. In fact, although the happy couple are the centre of attention, the day is not really about them at all. Weddings give their families and friends the opportunity to celebrate a new partnership, and to have a wonderful time.

As bridegrooms become more involved in organizing the wedding, they must come to terms with this simple fact: the people with the greatest expectations of the wedding are parents, relations and friends. For the happy couple, the wedding day is very hard work, and can be a real strain at times and the source of many hours' worry beforehand. As always the secret of overcoming this anxiety is good planning – and knowing what is expected of you. That is what this book is all about.

DECIDING AND PROPOSING

Despite the high divorce rate, marriage is still a popular institution and the chances are that most couples who find themselves in a steady, long-term relationship will opt to take the vows. That said, you may be subjected to great pressure from your girlfriend, and her or your family to tie the knot when you are perfectly happy as you are. One of the worst reasons to get married is because there is a baby on the way. A marriage forced on either of you in order to bring up a child is likely to be an unhappy and possible short-lived relationship, because both of you might have preferred a different partner.

WHY MARRY

If you are about to propose, or wondering why you haven't, try answering these questions:

1 Am I ready for the lifelong commitment of marriage?
2 Do we love each other?
3 Are my girlfriend and I compatible for marriage – can we be friends, lovers, advisers and supports to each other for the rest of our lives?
4 Do I want to start a family at some time? Would my partner want to?

5 Are there any subjects we never seem to agree on, and would these make marriage impossible (eg, you never agree about money, or have opposing views on starting a family, or one of you wants to work and live abroad)?

Obviously some of these questions require frank discussion between you both and others will make you delve into your own feelings. Compatibility does not mean to imply that you should be very similar people, but rather that you should mix together well.

It would be pretty difficult to go through a conversation prompted by the questions above and not either split up or become engaged. Assuming you both agree that you wish to plight your troths together, you can now propose! How you do this is up to you.

THE RIGHT DECISION

It is most important to be sure that you are completely happy with the decision, because the longer you harbour any lingering doubts, the more unhappy you will become, and the harder it will be to break off the engagement. Sometimes it is more difficult to be honest with yourself than to try to please other people by saying what they want to hear. Remember, this decision will affect the rest of both your lives.

ASKING PERMISSION

In times past, a suitor would ask the permission of his intended's father to marry his daughter. This practice has died out but you may wish to follow tradition and speak to your future father-in-law before formally proposing.

THE RING

Most women choose to show their engaged status by wearing a ring on the third finger of their left hand. The bridegroom pays for the ring, although it is generally chosen by both of you together. Engagement rings are usually set with precious stones. It is quite likely your fiancée will have a preference for which kind – perhaps she is one of the many who agree that diamonds are a girl's best friend, or she may prefer red rubies or a green emerald.

There is a wide choice available and it is best to visit several jewellers together before deciding. Costs vary, too, and it is as well to set an upper limit at the start to avoid the risk of disappointing your beloved later on by informing her that your finances cannot accommodate her tastes!

Whatever you choose, make sure you get a receipt. If the ring is expensive, your fiancée should add it to the

'all risks' section of her personal possessions insurance policy so that if it is lost, a replacement of equal value can be obtained.

Some couples opt not to buy an engagement ring (particularly if the wedding is to be quite soon) and may exchange some gifts instead, or put the money towards the honeymoon or their home. Some brides like to buy their fiancé an engagement present, perhaps a tie, a wallet, or even a ring – which would be worn on the third finger of the left hand.

ANNOUNCEMENTS

Once you are officially engaged, you must negotiate the potential minefield of who should be told first. Some people are terribly offended if they are told of an engagement after someone else has been – or, worse, hear the news from another party and not from the happy couple. This is particularly true of the older generation.

Your first priority is to tell both sets of parents and the rest of your families. This is best done verbally, either face to face or over the telephone. It is wise to consult your parents about whom they would like you to give the news to personally. Even if your family is very laid back on matters of etiquette, engagements and weddings seem to bring out the formal in everyone and you may be surprised at how keen your parents are for you to visit or ring certain relatives.

Stay calm – there is a lot more of this to come! It might be a good idea to make a list of the people whom you wish to know of your engagement. This will be the first of many such lists you will be preparing in the coming months.

You may wish to announce your engagement in your

local paper – especially if you have been living in the area for some time. You might even like to make an announcement in a national newspaper, which would be something to show your children in years to come! Make sure all your letters to friends and relations will have arrived prior to such an announcement appearing. To get the wording right, look at how other people have phrased their announcements in the relevant news-paper. You will find that companies which offer goods and services suitable for weddings also read these announcements, so you could receive a lot of extra mail from them!

CHECKLIST: engagement announcements

1 Parents and/or guardians
2 Close relations ⎫
3 Close friends ⎬ personally
4 Announcement at party ⎭
5 Letters to other family and friends
6 Advertisement in local/national newspaper

CHANGED RELATIONSHIPS

Once you are engaged, many things in your life will change. Friends who previously saw only one of you will begin to assume that the pair of you will be coming along for a drink, or to dinner. Of course people may have treated you both as an established couple for years, but you might notice your engagement has some effect on these friendships – you really are a 'couple' now.

IN-LAWS

It is one thing to meet the parents of a girlfriend, but quite another to meet your future in-laws. With luck, you will have seen them many times already and have established a friendly relationship. That should become even warmer as they welcome you fully into their family circle. If you have had less contact, or have not always hit it off, now is the time to make a lot of effort. When you visit them, be sure to take a gift – flowers or a bottle of wine – anything which they will appreciate and which shows that you are trying to be friendly.

As time goes on, try to keep that effort going. For instance, if your fiancée is writing to her parents, pop in a note yourself, perhaps to tell them whom you have chosen to be best man, or some other item of news which will interest them. Little gestures like this amount to more than one big gesture later on – you are building up a stock of goodwill.

If you have had little contact with your fiancée's parents (perhaps you live long distances apart, or your engagement has happened quickly, or there is some rift between daughter and parents), be as open as you can. Your fiancée will be able to brief you on what to expect. If she takes it for granted that you will remember the names of all her relations, write them out, possible in family chart form.

Her parents will naturally wish to know as much as possible about you: where you were born, your parents' occupations, the size of your family, your job, where you plan to live, and so on. However intrusive or irrelevant the questions, try to be tolerant. It never feels comfortable to be 'vetted', but in this case it is inevitable and your behaviour now is the foundation for an important future relationship.

If your relationship with your fiancée's parents has previously been uncomfortable, there is all the more reason to try to bury the hatchet now. Fathers are notoriously possessive of their daughters, and no boyfriend of hers seems able to win their approval. Try to understand this – if you have a daughter one day, you might end up feeling much the same! However, there is no harm in being quite blunt and saying 'I know we haven't really seen eye to eye before, but I hope we can learn to understand each other in the future.' Of course you will not use those exact words, and you may merely imply them by inviting your future father-in-law out for a drink, but if a rift worsens now, everyone will suffer – your fiancée and everyone connected with the wedding.

Most reasonable parents will respond to such overtures, and whatever the tensions of the past, they will want their daughter to be happy. If you make her this, her parents can ask for no more. Contrary to popular myth, fathers-in-law can be harder for a bridegroom to deal with than the frequently abused mother-in-law. Your fiancée may well find the opposite to be the case, hitting it off instantly with your delighted father while your mother sizes her up and decides whether she is the right woman to care for her son.

RELATIONSHIPS WITH EACH OTHER

Being aware of the various new pressures your relationship is now under, is essential at this time. When you attend family gatherings, you are often expected to behave as new lovers. You may not be new lovers in reality (you could have been lovers for years) but people like to see engaged couples in this light. Try to voice any disagreements in private, and present a united front in public.

BREAKING IT OFF

If one (or both) of you decides to break the engagement, any engagement gifts from friends and relations
should be returned. If you published an announcement
that you were to be married, you should make an
announcement in the same publication saying that the
wedding will not now take place. An offer should be
made to return any engagement rings which have been
given. With luck, the break-up will be amicable and you
will still be able to socialize with mutual friends, but
unfortunately this is not always the case.

ONCE YOU'RE ENGAGED

Being engaged is hard work. You are both helping to
organize the wedding, and preparing for your married
life, perhaps by buying or decorating your new home.
Somehow you seem to have to go to more family
occasions, taking your partner with you, and your busy
social life keeps going while you have a lot of other jobs
to do in planning your wedding.

Weddings are very good at creating disagreement.
You may suddenly discover that your vision of a quiet,
informal registry office wedding is quite unacceptable to
your fiancée, who has always wanted a church service
with all the 'trimmings'. Or you may both agree on the
kind of wedding you want, but find that her parents
have something quite different in mind, and, after all,
they are paying!

You may end up feeling you have very little choice in
the matter, and if you are prepared to go along with
what everyone else wants, this may not worry you
unduly. But if you are unhappy or uncomfortable with
the arrangements, a lot of tension could be created
between you and your bride. The best way forward is to
decide what would please you, and see how this fits in
with other people's views. You may have to compromise, but you should not be forced into a form of
wedding you do not like.

If you have recently attended a wedding (or, better
still, are about to go to one) think about how the day
went. Were the guests kept waiting a long time for

photographs? Did the speeches go on for too long? Think of anything that you particularly liked or disliked. Ask your married friends for any tips on the kind of problems they encountered and how they were solved.

WHAT KIND OF WEDDING DO YOU WANT?

The first decisions to be made are whether you wish to have a religious or a civil ceremony, and what sort of reception you and your bride want. Most church and registry office weddings take place on a Saturday, although they can take place on any other day of the week except a Sunday. Jewish weddings are held on a Sunday or a weekday, not on the Sabbath (Saturday).

CHURCH WEDDINGS

Getting married in church means you are taking part in a religious ceremony. It also generally implies a grand occasion attended by many friends and relations with the bride dressed in white and accompanied by several bridesmaids. Church weddings require a number of formalities (see page 32), and are usually held either at the bride's local church, or, if she now lives a long way from where she grew up, at her parents' local church, which would normally be the church of her parish. In addition to the religious implications, church weddings are generally much more of an 'event'.

REGISTRY OFFICE WEDDINGS

Registry offices are often located in local civic offices, and are therefore a good deal less aesthetically attractive than a church. Registry office weddings are usually on a smaller scale, with fewer guests and a fairly short ceremony. If you have a choice of registry offices to marry in (through your fiancée and your living in different districts) you might like to visit both first to see how they fit in with your plans. You may find the rooms are too small for the number of guests you would like to invite, or that the building would look awful in photographs.

SECOND MARRIAGES

If one or both of you are divorced you may have a little difficulty arranging a church wedding. The first thing to do is talk to the minister of the church of your choice. With luck, he will be perfectly happy to conduct a full service, provided that the decree absolutes can be produced. If he is not, there may be another local church where the minister has no such reservations. If this is not the case, or you do not wish to have a full church service, you could marry at a registry office and then have a short service of blessing in a church. This type of wedding is usually fairly informal, with a relatively small number of guests.

RECEPTIONS

In any case you will want to think about what kind of reception to hold after the wedding. This is in many ways the major part of the wedding, in the sense that it is where guests will spend most time, and will see most of the bride and bridegroom. Factors to consider include:

☆ Number of guests
☆ Venues available within easy reach of the wedding ceremony (hotels, other establishments with banqueting facilities such as museums or zoos; one popular

option is a marquee in the grounds of or near the bride's parents' home)
☆ Whether you want a formal sit-down meal or informal buffet
☆ The time of the wedding ceremony. If the service starts at noon, the guests will be hungry. If the wedding is in mid-afternoon, they will have had lunch and can wait longer for the next meal

Many couples choose to host an evening party after the reception, for close friends, young relations and perhaps some guests who could not be invited to the wedding service.

Whatever kind of wedding day you would prefer it may be affected by what others want, how much time you have for organizing the event, and how much you want to spend.

WHO PAYS FOR WHAT

The traditional breakdown of who pays for what in a church wedding is as follows:

Bride's father

☆ Press anouncements
☆ Bride's and bridesmaid's dresses
☆ Flowers for church and reception
☆ Photographer
☆ Most of the transport
☆ Wedding stationery
☆ The reception

The bridegroom

☆ Hire or cost of own clothes
☆ Costs at the church (except for flowers and service

sheets) – minister's fees, licence, organist, choir, and bell ringers
* Bouquets for bride and attendants
* Flower sprays for both mothers
* Buttonholes for self, best man and ushers
* Engagement and wedding rings
* Presents for attendants and best man
* Transport for self and best man to ceremony and self and bride to reception
* The honeymoon

In reality, the costs are often spread rather wider. This is partly because engaged couples now earning high salaries can afford to contribute much more than in previous generations. It is also a sign of a less regimented society where individuals have more of a say in what they would like to do.

Among the differences for a typical modern wedding would be:

* Bride buys own dress, and makes or buys brides-maids' dresses (although if these can be worn again, they or their parents may pay)
* Bride and bridegroom pay for press announcements and help with wedding stationery, postage and photography
* Ushers, if any, pay for hire of their suits
* Both families share cost of reception, or bride and bridegroom make a substantial contribution
* Bride and bridegroom share cost of honeymoon

The division of the expenses is not always easily settled. There can be a lot of negotiating and the bride and bridegroom can become caught up in any disagreements. If, say, the bridegroom's parents are far better off than the bride's, a contribution towards the costs seem fair. If, on the other hand, they are quite poor, the bridegroom should tactfully take their place as much as he can in any financial commitments that have to be made.

It is as well to know the total commitments early so that you know roughly how much to allow, and what you are asking the bride's father to pay. Although discussing money matters can be very tricky, if you are concerned, or feel he might be, try to raise the issue in a tactful way, such as 'I just wanted to make sure you were happy with the arrangements and aren't regretting the whole thing!'

Whoever is paying, when you add up how much can be spent on an event taking part of one day, the figures can be truly frightening and some couples decide that they do not wish their wedding to become a financial burden to others and opt either to pay for it all themselves (this is very much the norm when it is the bride's second marriage) or choose to have a wedding on a much smaller scale.

REGISTRY OFFICE

In the case of registry office weddings, the division of expenses is less defined. Much depends on the reason for choosing this venue. If a registry office is chosen because the couple do not want to be involved in a religious ceremony, the cost of the reception may be borne by the bride's parents, by both sets of parents, or split between them and the couple themselves. If it is a second marriage, the bride and groom generally meet all the expenses.

JEWISH WEDDINGS

Jewish weddings are generally organized on very traditional lines, and are usually paid for by the bride's parents.

STYLE OF DRESS

The bridegroom sets the tone on style of dress for male helpers and guests, and he may well choose to wear a suit. However, bridegrooms can be put under considerable pressure to wear morning dress. If you are unsure about what is appropriate, consult your in-laws, who will be able to tell you what is the usual style in their family.

It is also a good idea to talk to your parents about whether the guests from their side of the family would expect to wear morning dress – and are perhaps automatically assuming it is required and dusting off their own outfits. If they found on the day that they were dressed inappropriately, they could feel embarrassed. You may not like this kind of adherence to convention, but as was pointed out in the Introduction, weddings are about other people as well as yourself.

Full morning dress comprises:

1 Black morning coat
2 Grey striped trousers, without turn-ups
3 Grey waistcoat, generally double-breasted and with lapels
4 Grey tie
5 White shirt, turned-down collar
6 Black shoes and socks
7 White handkerchief in breast pocket
8 Grey (in times past, black) top hat with grey gloves

This is the most formal version and variations on it have become perfectly acceptable. The most popular one is a grey morning coat (which looks less forbidding and photographs better) and perhaps a cravat instead of a tie. Flamboyantly coloured cravats are acceptable at most weddings. For some reason the grey hat and gloves to match a grey morning coat have remained popular, although they are rarely worn and can be something of a nuisance as they have to be carefully carried everywhere. It is now quite common for the bridegroom to wear white, like his bride. This combination can be very striking.

If you are happy to wear a morning suit, you can hire or buy one. If you are likely to attend a number of formal weddings over the next few years, buying might be a worthwhile option, but otherwise hiring is much cheaper and is easily arranged.

You may be happy to dictate your vital statistics over the telephone when you order the outfit, but it is a sensible precaution to go to the hire shop for a fitting. Remember that the summer months are very popular for weddings, so you need to book as early as you can. Bear in mind also that hiring is usually done on a Friday to Monday basis, so you will need to arrange for the collection and return of the outfit.

THE ENGAGEMENT PARTY

Quite often one or two gatherings are held to celebrate your engagement. Such parties were once the occasion on which the engagement was officially announced, but today's guests are tipped off in advance on the cause for jubilation. The bride's parents have traditionally borne the cost of the event, but this habit is changing as the engaged couple themselves tend to take over the financing.

The venue is often the bride's parent's home, although if the two families live far apart, separate parties may be held at different times. If the bride and bridegroom live a long distance from both locations, they may choose to hold their own party wherever they live themselves.

Some couples use the engagement party as an

opportunity to entertain people who may not be able to come to the wedding itself, or who, because of restrictions on numbers, will not be invited to attend. Do make lists and consult your family about whom to invite – some relatives may be upset about being neglected in favour of friends from outside the family circle. Invitations are verbal, not written or printed.

The engagement party may be the first time that the bridegroom meets some of his fiancée's extended family. As when meeting his future in-laws, this can be a little intimidating and it is well worth making an extra effort with such people who will be part of his life from now on.

These gatherings are quite informal and might consist of drinks, or a light, buffet-style meal. The bride's father may make a short speech ending with a toast to the happy couple. The bridegroom replies by proposing the health of both sets of parents.

Even if you do not hold an engagement party, you should bring both sets of parents together as soon as is practical. If they have not met before, it might be worth keeping the meeting quite private away from other relations. These initial meetings can be a little tense as people who hardly know each other are under some pressure to get on. Their common ground is the bride and bridegroom, so be prepared to make a lot of the conversation and be the subject of much of the talk.

INTRODUCTIONS

You will be introducing many people to each other at such events, and it is worth remembering a few rules of etiquette on how to do this. Men are introduced to women, not the other way round, so you say 'Richard Boyle, meet Marian Foot'. Men generally stand up when being introduced to a woman. If one person is clearly older than the other, the rule to follow is that the younger one is introduced to the senior person. You may find it helpful to repeat the introduction the other way round to help your guests remember names, and perhaps add a little information about them. So you might say 'Peter Brittan, please meet my sister, Libby Diamond. Libby, this is Peter, my old school friend.' Try to use full names, not 'Mr' and 'Mrs'.

CHECKLIST: the engagement party

1 Decide on venue
2 Agree the date
3 Prepare a list of guests
4 Issue invitations
5 Order/prepare food and drink
6 Welcome guests
7 Make engagement announcement/speech
8 Ensure guests who require it have transport

THE BEST MAN

Your choice of best man is crucial to your – and other people's – enjoyment of the wedding. In many ways he will be more prominent at the reception than yourself, what with making speeches, helping people find their seats, acting as master of ceremonies, and so on. He will be your fellow-organizer, troubleshooter, friend, and will ensure you survive the stag party! It is therefore wise to decide who is to be your best man when you first begin to consider possible dates for your wedding. He can then also be involved in the preliminary arrangements.

CHOOSING THE BEST MAN

The best man is usually a single man who is your brother or your closest friend. On some rare occasions the 'best man' has been a woman; this adds a whole new element to the proceedings and will certainly surprise (and possibly delight) many of the wedding guests. This is the exception rather than the rule, however, and in this book it is assumed the best man is male.

Like it or not, your brother or closest friend may not be the perfect choice as best man. Perhaps he stutters terribly when asked to speak to a group of people, or is very forgetful and might not bring everything he needs on the day. Think your choice through carefully, for it will reflect on you – guests at a wedding do not base their judgements of the bridegroom solely on what they see of him; they also have a good look at his representative, the best man.

The following list notes the qualities required, in a rough order of importance:

☆ Capable of making a speech
☆ Reliable
☆ Well organized
☆ Unflappable
☆ Acceptable to the bride's family
☆ Good with people

The speech is at the top of the list because it is the most public of his duties and the one the best man will be remembered for. You can, if you choose, work together on your speeches (there is a whole chapter devoted to them, see pages 86–90) but you must be confident that your best man will not 'freeze' on the day.

The other qualities are required because the best man plays an important role in behind-the-scenes organization, and is central to the smooth running of proceedings on the big day.

CHECKLIST: Best man's duties at church wedding

1 Arranges and pays for own outfit and checks that bridegroom and ushers have done same
2 Helps to organize stag party
3 Keeps in touch with bride's family about arrangements
4 Checks ushers' buttonholes and the service sheets at the church
5 Accompanies bridegroom into church and sits beside him
6 Pays any necessary dues at the church on behalf of the bridegroom

7 Hands ring to minister or priest at appropriate moment

8 Ensures all guests have transport to reception venue

9 Ensures bridegroom's going-away clothes are taken to reception venue

10 Acts as master of ceremonies at reception (unless another guest has been given this role)

11 Announces speeches and cutting of cake

12 Makes speech at reception on behalf of bridesmaids

13 Ensures going-away car is decorated, but not incapacitated

14 Returns suits if they were hired

The checklist clearly shows that in addition to being the bridegroom's minder, the best man has a number of organizational duties. Once you have selected the person you feel is best equipped to handle the job, sound him out. He might reel in terror at the very idea, or have been best man so many times that he is thoroughly fed up with the role, and would prefer to have less responsibility by being an usher.

Don't be offended if he refuses – think whether you would do the job yourself, and what reservations might enter your head. Have a second choice in mind and be honest with him: 'I asked Mike first because I've known him since we were kids, but he just doesn't feel he can do it, and I think you would be brilliant.'

When he has accepted the honour, the best man should be introduced to the chief bridesmaid as soon as possible, since they will work together quite a lot in their duties, each performing a similar role for the bridegroom and the bride respectively.

JEWISH CEREMONIES

The best man at a Jewish ceremony is usually of the same faith, and often one of the bridegroom's brothers.

If he has none, a close male relative is generally chosen. In addition to the duties at other types of religious ceremony, the best man may help the bridegroom to practise reciting in Hebrew. If top hats are not being worn, skullcaps must be worn in the synagogue. After the ceremony, the best man hands any fees including travelling expenses to the rabbi and the cantor (singer), in sealed envelopes.

NON-CONFORMIST CEREMONIES

Non-conformist, such as Quaker, ceremonies are much more informal, and a best man (or bridesmaid) is rarely chosen.

USHERS

One of the first things you and your best man will decide is the choice of ushers (if there are to be any). Their chief role is to show guests to their seats in church, hand out service sheets or hymn books, and help to organize transport to the reception. One may be put in charge of overseeing car parking at the reception venue. Since they will be directing guests, it is clearly an advantage if they know many of them (as ushers drawn from your families are bound to) so that they do not constantly have to ask 'bride or groom' at the church entrance.

The ushers traditionally escort the bridesmaids from the church, so you will need to check with your fiancée on how many bridesmaids there are to be. For most reasonably large church weddings, six or eight ushers are required. They should be unmarried men chosen from among your friends, and both families – it is important that suitable men in your bride's family are offered the honour of the role.

Sometimes one man is appointed chief usher and leads the team. This is particularly usual when the best man is based a long way away and will only be free to take up his duties the day before the wedding. In this case, the bridegroom may select another good friend to take on some of the best man's preliminary duties, and ask him to accept the role of chief usher. The chief usher escorts the bride's mother and the bridegroom's parents to their seats.

Once you have chosen your ushers, they must be told:

☆ the date and location of the wedding
☆ what they will be expected to wear (suits or morning dress, see page 21)

OTHER ATTENDANTS

Any other attendants you would like are also chosen at this stage. Your fiancée and her parents will probably be the chief decision-makers on which ones to have.

☆ Bridesmaids – preferably chosen from both families. Check with your family whether there are any suitable girls or young women who would like to be asked. If necessary a chief bridesmaid can keep an eye on very young assistants
☆ Page boys – usually two, if any, and chosen from either family
☆ Matron of honour (if any – chosen by the bride)
☆ Master of ceremonies – to announce speeches and generally keep things moving at the reception. This is an excellent role for an older member of the family – perhaps an uncle. He could help to deter frivolous souls who may be planning some mischief such as hiding fish to rot in the bridegroom's car

It is important to make these arrangements early, and explain to the people concerned exactly what you will be asking them to do. It would be a good idea to supply them with a checklist of their responsibilities and points such as dress code. They might josh you about being bureaucratic, but they will appreciate the information and you will feel relieved that they know what is expected of them.

THE LEGAL SIDE

The bride and bridegroom must take care of a number of legal formalities well in advance of the wedding ceremony whether this is to be a religious or civil one. Some of these require several weeks' notice so it is prudent to plan ahead and ensure that all necessary steps have been taken before the busy last month or two.

ENGLAND AND WALES

In these countries a marriage can take place at a civil ceremony, a Church of England ceremony, or in accordance with the rites of any other religious denomination.

CHURCH OF ENGLAND

Marriage here can be authorized in any of four ways:

a) Publication of banns
b) Common (ordinary) licence
c) Special licence
d) With a licence issued by a superintendent registrar

a) Publication of banns
This is the most popular method, and involves the notice of your impending marriage being read out in a

church in both the bridegroom's and bride's parishes. You must first contact the minister of the church where you would like the marriage to take place and ask for his permission to hold the service. If you both live within that parish, that is all you need to do. If not, you should both also visit the minister of the church in the parish where the other one of you lives.

Each minister arranges for your marriage banns to be read aloud in the relevant church on three successive Sundays before the wedding ceremony. A small charge is made for doing this. It is customary for the engaged couple to attend at least one of the services when the banns are read.

If you and your fiancée live in different parishes, the minister in whose church you are not getting married will sign a certificate confirming that the banns have been called. Without it, his counterpart cannot perform the wedding service, so make sure you pick the certificate up in good time.

If one of the couple is a serving member of the Royal Navy at sea, the banns can be read by the chaplain or ship's captain, and a certificate stating that no objection has been raised must be provided.

Incidentally, check your birth certificate before visiting the minister, and make sure you know what your full legal name is. You may find to your surprise that you have one or two middle names you were never aware of, or even that the name you are known by is not your official first name. This is important as the banns should include all the names shown on your birth certificate, and if appropriate, any other name by which you are usually known. If you discover an embarrassing middle name now, you must get used to it, because your full name has to be read out at the marriage ceremony. If you think it is going to cause sniggering in the congregation, tell people about it beforehand – it will be easier to handle all round!

b) Common licence

This is a much quicker procedure in which the residential requirement is that one of you must have lived in the area served by the church to be used for the ceremony for at least 15 days prior to the application. Banns are not read and the licence is issued the next day. This is a good standby if there has been a slip-up and it is too late to read the banns.

These licences can be obtained from the local surrogate (who may be the minister himself, and if not he can advise whom you should contact) or by visiting the Faculty Office, 1 The Sanctuary, Westminster, London SW1. The applicant must sign a declaration that there is no legal reason for the marriage not to take place, and that either party fulfils the residential requirements.

c) Special licence

This is an unusual method in which a licence is issued from the Faculty Office by the Archbishop of Canterbury, but only when there is some special, urgent reason why other methods cannot be used.

d) Superintendent Registrar's Certificate

Another rarity, this certificate is issued by the superintendent registrar for the district in which the marriage will take place, and must be applied for at least 21 days ahead of the wedding date.

OTHER DENOMINATIONS

If one partner is a Roman Catholic and the service is to be held in an Anglican (or other) church, the marriage is called a 'mixed marriage'. Such marriages can only take place in one church, not both. The Roman Catholic church used to excommunicate its members for marrying in a non-Roman Catholic church, but the rules today are more relaxed. A bride and bridegroom of differing religions are expected to meet a priest or minister of both faiths and learn something of the other's beliefs. Some Catholic priests may expect a series of informal discussions in which the Catholic partner promises to guard his or her faith and bring any children up in it.

Marriages between two people of differing Protestant and non-conformist denominations are less complicated, although obviously the minister will wish to be informed of both parties' beliefs. The real problems start when one partner is a declared non-Christian – in which case it would be very difficult to persuade a minister or priest to allow the ceremony to be held in an Anglican or Catholic church.

If you both hold strong, but different beliefs, you will probably have discussed these together many times before. Although you may well be able to tolerate each other's beliefs, it can be much harder to agree in what faith any children you have should be brought up. If it becomes an issue between you, you could seek counselling from representatives of either (or both) faiths, but do allow time to consider this important point.

JEWISH WEDDING

A marriage within Jewish rites can only take place between two Jews, and some documentation proving their faith may be required. Under Civil Law, all marriages must take place before a Superintendent Registrar of Marriages. For Jews, this marriage can be held ahead of the Jewish religious service, or directly after it, at the synagogue. The latter is only possible when the synagogue's Minister or Secretary is recognized as a Registrar's representative.

REGISTRY OFFICE WEDDINGS

If you opt to marry in a registry office you will need to contact the local superintendent registrar. His address can be found in the telephone directory under the heading 'Registration of Births, Deaths and Marriages'. The superintendent registrar will arrange the marriage in one of three ways:

a) Certificate
b) Certificate and Licence
c) Registrar General's Licence

a) Certificate

This is arranged from a form giving the names, addresses and ages of those who wish to be married, together with where the wedding is to take place. If either party is under 18, a declaration that the parents' consent has been given is also required. The official then makes an entry in his notice book, and issues the certificate 21 days later – valid for three months from the original notice book entry.

If the couple have lived in the district controlled by the registrar for at least seven days, only one of them need appear to make the declaration. If not, each must visit their respective district registrars, and be able to show that they have lived in that district for seven days prior to the visit.

b) Certificate and Licence

This follows a similar procedure, except the residential qualifications are different. One person must have lived in the district for 15 days prior to the application. Their partner must normally reside in England or Wales, and does not need to visit a registrar.

The licence is issued one clear day after the application.

c) Registrar General's Licence

This is an unusual method used when one party is

seriously ill and cannot be moved. The other partner must visit the local superintendent registrar to obtain a certificate or licence, but residential conditions and waiting periods are waived.

SCOTLAND

The days of couples eloping to Gretna Green in Scotland to get married with two witnesses taken from the street are over, but the rules in Scotland are still different from England and Wales. Banns are not required to be read, and both parties must obtain a marriage notice form from a registrar of births, deaths and marriages, and inform the registrar for the district in which the ceremony is to take place. The minimum notice period is 15 days.

The following documents are required in addition to the marriage notice:
1 Birth certificate
2 If the marriage is not your or your bride's first, a copy of the divorce decree or annulment, or the death certificate of the former spouse
3 If either party lives outside the United Kingdom, a certificate of no impediment to marriage

If any of this paperwork is not written in English, a certified translation is required.

After this, a date can be confirmed for either a civil or religious marriage.

NORTHERN IRELAND

In Northern Ireland notice to marry should be made to the District Registrar of Marriages, and the residence qualification is seven days. Marriage may take place by: licence, special licence, banns, certificate from a registrar or licence from a district registrar of marriage.

MARRYING ABROAD

Some couples choose to marry far from their own country, and spend their honeymoon in some possibly exotic location. The number of guests would obviously be very restricted, as it would be expensive for them to attend such a wedding. Requirements are different in every country, so you must find out what documentation will be required to ensure the marriage is legal. The minimum is probably your birth certificates, proof of residence, and a certificate showing that there is no impediment to the marriage. Make an early visit to the foreign consul of the country concerned to find out what you have to do.

SECOND MARRIAGES

Second marriages are fairly common today, reflecting the high divorce rate. Remember that neither party can re-marry until the decree absolute has been granted. Widows and widowers can marry in a church or synagogue. Divorcees may find the church of their choice declines to marry them (this applies particularly to Anglican churches and invariably in Catholic churches).

PRACTICALITIES

This chapter deals with a few of the nitty-gritty aspects of planning a wedding. As bridegroom, you may not feel very involved in them – until someone asks you a question, and you realize you should be taking a keen interest in everything that is going on!

There may be times when you have the feeling that all your wedding is about is lists. You'd be right – it should be. For if something is not on a list, it could be forgotten, and there is nothing worse than finding that out on the day. Can your Aunt Annie manage the steps to the reception venue? Do you want any photographs taken in advance of the big day? When will the ring be ready? All details, maybe, but as the bridegroom, you are at the centre of proceedings, and you need to be involved.

INVITATIONS

This is one of the trickiest areas of any wedding. No matter how generous the numbers seem at first, by the time all the 'musts' have been written down, it often seems as if you will need a church and reception venue twice the size of the chosen ones!

Start by finding out the capacity of the place in which the ceremony is to be held. How many people will it comfortably seat? (Don't count the pew where you and the best man will sit.) The guest list can be divided into seven sections:

1 Bride's core family
2 Bridegroom's core family
3 Bride's other relations
4 Bridegroom's other relations
5 Bride and bridegroom's friends
6 Bride's parents' friends
7 Local 'musts'

The final two categories may be a surprise to the bridegroom, but if the bride's parents are bearing most of the cost of the wedding, it is probably on their 'patch', and they run the risk of offending a lot of local people if they cannot invite them. In a sense, they are hosting a party being held in your honour, to which you are allowed to invite some of your friends. Included in the local 'musts' if it is a church wedding is the minister conducting the service.

DIVORCED PARENTS

Some tact is required if either, or both, sets of parents are divorced or separated. In the bride's case, the invitations are extended in the name of the parent she lives with, or last lived with. It is up to the bridegroom whether both his divorced parents should be invited. In such cases it is common for them both to bury the hatchet for the day and attend, although the presence of any new partners can bring a certain amount of tension. You really have to trust them to consider your feelings and behave pleasantly on the day.

Another tricky point relates to whether you want young children and babies at the ceremony. They can be noisy and disruptive. On the other hand, weddings are a celebration of family life, and it seems a shame to exclude them. If you do want to avoid the risk of bored children or tired babies interrupting the ceremony, tactfully explain that you would welcome them at the reception but not at the service. Even at the reception, however, children can become restless and badly behaved, and may be occupying a seat at the same expense as an adult. If a lot of your friends and relations have young children, you could consider hiring several childminders and running a creche throughout the day.

Both bride and bridegroom should write down every member of their family who really must be invited. Consult both sets of parents about any relations who should be on the list. Continue through the rest of the categories, until you have the full list. Counting up, you are quite likely to find you have too many names. Now you have to be quite ruthless and put together an 'A' and 'B' list – the 'B's being a set of substitutes. They can be invited if people on the 'A' list decline the invitation, and/or can be asked to the reception, but not the wedding ceremony.

Even if your fiancée and her parents are organizing the wedding virtually single-handed, make sure you have your say now because if you miss out someone from your side of the family, it could cause a lot of resentment all round. The invitations are sent out by the bride's parents, and replies are addressed to them.

Invitations are usually sent out 6–8 weeks before the wedding. Sometimes they are issued much earlier, and in many instances the engaged couple help by address-ing envelopes and sending out their own batch. It is sensible to include directions for finding the church or registry office and the reception venue, in words and with a map. A list of accommodation with addresses and telephone numbers might be appreciated by guests living far away. If close family are able to stay with the bride's relations, this should also be made clear.

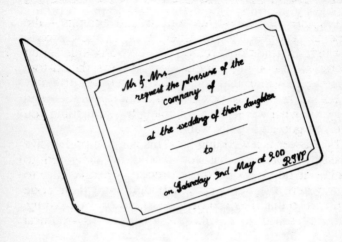

Mr & Mrs _____
request the pleasure of the
company of _____

at the wedding of their daughter

_____
to
_____

on Saturday 2nd May at 2.00   RSVP

If an 'A' and 'B' list is being used, ensure that if necessary people are chased up for a reply, so that if there are any refusals, someone from the second group may be invited. This is a complicated and time-consuming business, but there is no way of avoiding it.

Remind your friends and relations that they should reply promptly to say whether or not they can come. If names from your list are slow responding it could embarrass you in front of your future in-laws.

Once all the replies have been received, a table plan will be prepared if there is to be a sit-down meal. You may like to mix friends and relations together so that they get to know each other, or to seat guests with people they already know. If any guests do not get on, make this known so that they can be kept apart.

THE WEDDING LIST

This is one of the real fun aspects of weddings – the presents! People like to offer gifts to newly-weds. Although the traditional reason – to help a couple set up a home from nothing – applies less and less, the custom has remained. Because you and your fiancée probably have a fair number of possessions already, people need advice on what would be a suitable gift – something you have not got, and really want.

The answer is a wedding list. This is a comprehensive breakdown of gifts that you would be delighted to receive. It needs to be quite precise – people like to know where the items can be bought, and their code numbers so that they can be sure to buy the right thing. It makes sense to break the list into geographical sections, according to where most of the guests live:

1 Items available in the bride's parents area
2 Items available in the bridegroom's parents' area
3 Items available in the area(s) where the bride and bridegroom live

You will need to put more things on the list than you expect to receive, so that people have a wide choice. The best approach is to visit shops in each area together, picking out things you want, and ensuring that you select items in a broad price range. Many large stores offer a service whereby they keep a list of the items you have chosen, so that you can simply tell would-be present-buyers to ask to see what you still need.

'Shopping' for the wedding list is refreshing because you can choose things simply because you like them, not as to whether you can afford them yourselves. Don't get carried away! Think about what you may need not only for your home, but, for example, there may be a sport you play together for which you would like new equipment. Prepare the list at the same time as the guest list, so that it can be quickly despatched to those who request it. You and your bride can keep a record of who intends to buy what – or her mother may wish to do so. You may find you start to receive gifts as soon as the list is sent out, as people may prefer not to bring their presents on the day. Even if you see the giver the next day and thank them, always write a thank you letter and make a note of what they have given you.

Sometimes presents are displayed at the reception, so you may wish to keep all your gifts pristine for this. Note down who sent a cheque, so that their names can be written on a card (without mentioning the actual sums given) to be included in the display.

RINGS

A visit to a jeweller's shop is also essential: to buy your bride's ring, and possibly choose one for yourself if you wish. Bridegrooms are increasingly opting to have a wedding ring, too, often in a design which complements that of the bride's ring.

Wedding rings are usually made in platinum, white gold (9 or 18 carat) or yellow gold (9, 18 or 22 carat). The lower the carat number, the less pure gold there is, making the ring harder and less lustrous, but costing less. White gold is so soft it is not used in 22-carat form, and over the years it wears away and loses some of its original bright sheen.

It is a good idea to look at wedding rings when you are buying the engagement ring, as your partner will wear them both on the third finger of her left hand and they should complement each other. That does not mean you have to buy them at the same time, but you may be able to form some idea of what you want the wedding ring to be like when you purchase the engagement one.

You have a choice of three sources for the ring(s):

a) a jeweller's shop
b) an antique shop
c) a jewellery designer

a) Jeweller's shop

Whatever your choice, your first stop should be a reputable jeweller. You will be able to see a wide range of rings, which will help you to identify your likes and dislikes, and obtain some idea of cost which can vary enormously. An assistant will assess the size of ring needed. Size codings are by letter, and the ring(s) you choose may require adjustment to fit.

b) Antique shops

Quite a few couples like the idea of buying rings with a little history, and it can be fun to take pot luck and look in antique shops for a secondhand (literally!) ring. Such rings are sometimes significantly cheaper than their brand new equivalents. If it does not fit, a good jeweller will be able to adjust the size. If it is tarnished, again a jeweller will be able to polish it up.

c) Jewellery designer

For a unique ring, find a jewellery designer to make up your own special one. Browse round the shops first to get an idea of what you like, then discuss the material, design and price with the designer. Some couples find this process particularly satisfying as they can put a lot of effort and thought into creating a ring which expresses their attachment. Costs are higher than from jeweller's shops, but you can of course set a budget for the designer.

ARRANGING THE CHURCH SERVICE

Another important job requiring advance planning in which the bridegroom should be involved is arranging the church service. Sheets are usually printed with the order of service and words of the hymns, and the text must be given to the printer in good time to ensure they will be ready. You might have a favourite hymn (perhaps one from your schooldays or from some other time with fond memories). It will make the service more individual if you can include at least one of these.

Still on the musical theme, do you want music played while you are out of view signing the register or a hymn sung? You may have friends who can form a quartet and play, or you may want a special piece of organ music. Whatever you wish, make it clear early so that, say, the quartet can rehearse, or the organist can be sure he or she has a copy of the relevant music.

As for the rest of the service, most of it comes in standard form, but brides are often given a choice of whether they want to state that they will 'obey' their husbands (you might have differing views on this!).

PHOTOGRAPHER

Whether or not to have a professional photographer at a wedding is a decision too often given little thought. The tendency is to hire the local photographer and ask for a standard set of pictures. But many a wedding has been, while not exactly ruined, certainly made less joyful, by bossy cameramen who dominate proceedings from the moment you leave the church or registry office. They keep everybody waiting and often produce pictures that look as if you were all being passed along on a conveyor belt!

The best answer is to bring in a real professional – meaning someone well organized and very good with people – preferably on a personal recommendation. However, you could ask a few of your friends to take some pictures. This choice is cheaper and can make a lot of sense. With today's camera technology enabling just about anyone to take shots of a reasonable standard, there are in fact many enthusiasts who are really very good photographers. Pick, say, three friends and give them a generous supply of film. Give one of them a list of the shots that you definitely want taken, for example:

1 The bride and bridegroom
2 The happy couple with both sets of parents
3 Bridegroom, best man and ushers
4 Bride and bridesmaids
5 The happy couple with relatives

All these can be taken after the ceremony. You may want a few other standard shots such as the bridegroom and best man arriving, the bride and her father arriving, and the bride and bridegroom going away. But you should also encourage your friends to take photographs of individuals and groups enjoying the occasion. Very often a shot of people watching the formal photographs being taken is much more natural than the 'set up' shot itself! In general people in photographs look much nicer looking at each other or at an angle, rather than beaming glassily straight into the lens.

After the wedding, retrieve all the films for processing. With a bit of work you will be able to put together a marvellous sequence showing the key people interspersed with other friends and relatives – a much nicer memento than the strait-laced, standard shots.

If you opt to use a professional, supply an advance list of the shots you definitely want him or him to take, and agree a price. Even with this arrangement, it will do no harm to supply films to friends as an alternative source of pictures.

You may like to give a specially prepared album or framed print to both sets of parents, as well as filling an album with your favourite photographs for yourselves.

DO YOU WANT A VIDEO?

In addition to a photographer (and occasionally as an alternative) some couples hire a video firm to film the big day. The production company produces an edited 'programme' showing key events, accompanied by appropriate music. Opinions vary as to the value of these videos. They do provide a moving, rather than static, record of the day, and filming arrivals and departures from the ceremony and reception will ensure that everyone involved in the wedding is preserved on tape. However, before booking a video company you should first check that the minister has no objections, and then ask yourselves the following questions:

1 Can we (or the bride's father) afford it?
2 How often would we actually watch the video?
3 How much disruption and inconvenience would the film-makers inevitably cause during the day?

The last question can be discussed with potential suppliers, but think back to any weddings you have attended which were filmed. The mere presence of a camera and lights tends to inhibit guests, and can slow the sequence of events. The other two questions are obviously quite subjective. If you have relations or friends in other parts of the world who cannot attend, they might be very pleased to receive a video of the day.

Incidentally, as with cameras, the latest camcorders allow easy video filming in all kinds of light and often with automatic focusing. If you have a friend who is skilled in their use, he or she may be able to put together an amateur video with which you would be perfectly happy.

PRESENTS

There are a number of people to whom the bride and bridegroom may like to give presents on the day of the wedding:

1 Bride's parents
2 Bridegroom's parents
3 Bridesmaids
4 Best man
5 Others who have made a special contribution – perhaps a friend made the bride's dress, or a relative arranged all the flowers in the church or decorated the cake, or the ushers.

These will be presented at some stage in the reception. Bouquets are a popular choice for the women recipients, but put your heads together to think of something for each person which they will really cherish as a souvenir of the occasion. Write a personal thank you on the accompanying card.

While discussing presents for parents, one very nice gesture is to write the week before the wedding, thanking them for all they are doing on your behalf and telling them how much you are both looking forward to the day. This adds to the store of goodwill all round.

ACCOMMODATION

If close friends or relations live a long way from the wedding venue, they may need help in locating accommodation. Firstly, find out if the bride's local family and friends can offer hospitality, and try to match like-minded or similarly aged people. Otherwise, and for other friends, supply a list of local accommodation and leave it up to them.

TRANSPORT

If some guests do not have a car or have particular transport needs (for example, if they are disabled), try to make any necessary arrangements for lift-giving early on and keep everybody informed. You should also be thinking about your own transport. How will you be getting to the ceremony, and how will you and your bride leave for the reception? A popular option is for the happy couple to depart in the car which brought the bride and her father to the church or registry office. If this is the case, make sure your own car does not get stranded!

PLANNING THE HONEYMOON

The bridegroom traditionally arranges the honeymoon, sometimes keeping its location secret from his bride so that she enjoys a genuine surprise when she discovers where they are going. The honeymoon is likely to be your major holiday of the year – unless you had already booked one at some other time, in which case you may be restricted to having as little as a week or even a few days for your honeymoon. For this reason, you may like to discover from your fiancée if there is a special place she has always wanted to visit.

A wealth of travel packages is available, some catering specifically for honeymooners. You may choose to fly to somewhere sunny and relaxing, or to visit romantic cities such as Paris, Venice or Vienna. Perhaps you just want to book a few days in a luxurious hotel, or spend a week at a country club or on an activity break, learning to windsurf or ride, for example.

The choice is wide, but bear in mind the following:
1 If you are travelling abroad, both of you need valid passports. If your bride wishes to change hers to her married name, she will need to fill in a form obtainable from the Post Office and send it in at least six weeks before the wedding. The form must be signed by the person who is to officiate at the ceremony. You may also need injections to immunize you against tropical diseases.
2 Even if you keep the destination a secret from your bride, she will appreciate knowing what climate to expect and how formal/informal the location will be, so that she can pack the right clothes.

3 You may be facing the expense of setting up a new home, which is very costly. Be sure you can afford the holiday you are planning – you could always splash out next year if you hold back this time.

4 Many hotels offer special terms for honeymooners and will appreciate being told in advance that you have just got married – this will invariably be to your advantage, for people like to make their own contribution to the happiness of such a special time!

5 Practical jokers, however, love disrupting honeymoons by cancelling bookings or 'hiding' tickets: it is therefore prudent to limit how many people know your destination.

6 You may prefer to stay locally on your first night, so that you can remain at the reception until late, or return for the evening party.

THE STAG PARTY

When your engagement is announced, one of the first questions male friends and relatives will ask you is the date of the stag party. Apart from turning up at the church on time, holding a stag party seems to be one of the bridegroom's most important jobs! However, if a stag night does not appeal to you, be bold and say so. This may result in a certain number of raised eyebrows, not to mention howls of disappointment, but it is more important that you are true to yourself. Equally, as it is your wedding, you can control what form a stag party would take, and this might enable you to overcome any reservations about having one.

The traditional stag party was an all-male drinking session held in a local hostelry the night before the wedding, culminating in various high-jinks including (occasionally) such cruel acts as placing the incapacitated bridegroom on an express train. The modern party is different in several ways:

✩ The event is held days, or even weeks, ahead of the actual wedding, for the convenience of the guests and to ensure the bridegroom arrives at the wedding in a fit state to get through a gruelling day
✩ The venue can be anywhere conveniently reached by all the guests – sometimes even in another country
✩ Rather than a night's carousing, the celebration might take up a whole day or even a weekend, and have a theme, such as a day playing a certain sport

The stag night remains, however, a resolutely all-male affair, in which the bridegroom's friends and relations mark the end of his days of bachelorhood and console him at the prospect of entering the married state. Needless to say, humour plays a central part in the proceedings.

Although the stag night is theoretically organized by the best man, in fact the bridegroom usually has a large role to play and if his best man lives far away, he might take on the whole job. You must first decide what form the event will take:

1 How long the event should last: an evening, a day, a weekend.
2 The form of entertainment you wish to include – for example, go to a show, have a meal, or spend a day stock car racing. You might decide on a gathering in a private room in a pub or hotel, or meeting there before moving on to other entertainment. Or meeting in a wine bar or restaurant for a meal.

The range of activities you could choose is very wide. Perhaps you could all go ten-pin bowling, hire a canal boat for a weekend, or enjoy a day's water skiing? One popular choice is a day of 'paint wars', when groups split up into teams and fire paint pellets at each other in a 'battle zone'. The day might conclude with a snooker or pool tournament. Another option that has developed in recent years is a stag weekend in which the entire group travels to another country for a sightseeing trip.

Once you have decided on what kind of event yu want, draw up a list of whom you wish to invite. The traditional guest list would include only unmarried men, but this custom has fallen by the wayside and the guests can include any male friends and relations, generally of about the same age as yourself. Make a point of inviting your bride's brothers, even if you do not know them well, as it is a friendly gesture and if they do come, you can become better acquainted.

Invitation is informal and can be done by telephone or letter. You will need to know responses pretty soon as you may need to confirm numbers with the venue hosting the event. If there is a cost per head, this should be made clear from the beginning. Some guests travelling long distances might appreciate accommodation being arranged, either at the home of another guest, or at a hotel. Find out and book early. It is wise to request any necessary payments in advance, avoiding any embarrassing 'chasing up' just before the wedding.

If the location is unfamiliar, maps and directions should be sent to all guests in advance. As the bridegroom you should get there early, accompanied by the best man, to welcome your guests.

There is no compunction for the bridegroom to pay for a round of drinks for all his guests. Indeed, the best man may organize for the bridegroom's expenses to be met collectively by the other guests, but don't bank on it! However, speeches might be called for. These are made only by the best man and the bridegroom, and should be highly informal. The best man might console the bridegroom on the ending of his days as a carefree, single man, and congratulate him on avoiding the married state for so long. The bridegroom might reply in a tone of mock-sorrow, pointing out that he has been trapped into the marriage. Keep it brief and amusing. See pages 86–90 for advice on planning and making a speech.

At the end of the evening, the bridegroom and the best man should ensure that all guests have taxis available to take them home, unless there is convenient public transport, and should be the last to leave.

CHECKLIST: The stag party

1 Select venue/events
2 Choose the date
3 Set a budget, for yourself if you are paying, or per head if you are to ask for contributions
4 Prepare lists of guests
5 Issue invitations
6 Arrange accommodation if necessary
7 Welcome your guests
8 Make a short speech at some stage
9 Ensure all guests have departed safely, in taxis if necessary
10 Thank the best man

THE REHEARSAL AND WEDDING

Your wedding day should be one of the happiest and most memorable of your life. It will certainly be quite hard work.

One of the remarkable aspects of a wedding is that it is very likely to be the first and only time that a sizeable proportion of the bride and bridegroom's relatives and friends find themselves under one roof. They too should enjoy the occasion and will certainly have more opportunities than you to talk to old friends and meet new ones. In front of them, you will state your commitment to your bride, and with them you will celebrate your mutual love.

ON THE EVE OF THE WEDDING

The final preparations for the wedding start the day before.

THE REHEARSAL FOR A CHURCH WEDDING

It is customary, and certainly very sensible, to arrange for a rehearsal of the ceremony the day before the event, particularly if you having a big wedding. You will need to arrange this with the minister or priest and the other parties – the bride's father, the best man and if possible the bridesmaids and at least one usher.

Although the atmosphere might be quite relaxed, do pay close attention to anything the minister or priest says about where you should stand and in what order events will happen. You can dress informally but make a mental note of, for example, where you would put your hat or gloves if you are carrying them, or where you might rest a prayer book.

The rehearsal might inspire you to learn your lines if you have not already done so. The minister or priest usually asks you to repeat his words when the time comes to give your vows. Some display the words on a card facing you, suspended from their service book. However, learning your lines will enable you to deliver them much more confidently.

Some couples actually ask the minister or priest not to prompt them as they wish to recite their vows on their own. This gives a very nice 'feel' to this important part of the service, communicating the couple's commitment to each other through their confidence. If you choose to do this, inform the minister or priest (who may have reservations) and keep a card with the words clearly printed on it with you at the altar just in case nerves get the better of you.

JOBS FOR THE WEDDING EVE

Check that all the items you are responsible for have been prepared and either delivered or collection arranged. These include:

☆ The order for buttonholes which often goes to the supplier of other flowers. Are there enough ordered for both fathers, the ushers, the best man, yourself and any other people who have requested them?

☆ If you have hired a morning suit, you need to pick it up and check it is complete. Try it on: are any alterations necessary? Check that your shoes are clean and your shirt ironed. Keep the entire outfit together in a wardrobe.

☆ Are all the taxis ordered?

If you intend to use your car for transport the next day, you will want to wash it, check oil and water levels, and fill up with petrol (nothing could be worse than running out on the way to the service!).

It is also worth getting hold of a curtain or similar ring just in case there is a disaster with the wedding ring the next day. The knowledge of that back-up in your pocket will do a lot to relax you!

In case you do not have time the next day, you will also need to pack your going-away clothes to change into after the reception, and your case for the honeymoon, together with all necessary documents including travellers' cheques, tickets and passport. It is also wise to give the best man any monies required for church fees which he is expected to pay tomorrow on your behalf. These should be in sealed envelopes with the name of the recipient clearly marked.

You will doubtless be called on to do various other jobs for the bride's mother, such as carrying guests' cases, and picking up and delivering the cake. It's going to be a busy day!

CHECKLIST: eve of wedding

1 Check going-away attire
2 Pack going-away clothes
3 Pack honeymoon luggage
4 Check wedding attire
5 Buttonholes delivered?
6 Wedding ring and substitute ring safe?

7 Money for church fees obtained from bank?
8 Taxis ordered?
9 Car checked?
10 Ushers briefed?

EVENING ENTERTAINMENT

Assuming you have wisely chosen to hold your stag party well ahead of the wedding, you will be free on the evening prior to the big day. If both sets of parents are in the area, it might be nice for you to have a meal together. This will help to strengthen the bond between the two families.

As it is supposedly bad luck for the bridegroom and bride to meet on the wedding day before the service, you will be staying in separate houses – perhaps at a hotel with your parents, and preferably under the same roof as the best man who should, of course, be included in any evening entertainment along with other special friends such as the chief bridesmaid. By all means celebrate, but remember that you don't want a hangover tomorrow.

THE MORNING

Being away from the hectic activity of the bride's parent's home, the bridegroom's wedding morning can be a fairly relaxed affair. You want to look and feel your best: sleep late if you can, and have a good breakfast. Shave carefully (cuts and plasters will haunt you in the wedding photographs for years otherwise!). It is a better idea to shave normally twice rather than try to do one extra thorough shave. Have a bath or shower, and make sure your hair has no stray 'antennae' sticking out.

If the wedding is in the afternoon, you have the morning to enjoy, but otherwise you will need to get dressed in your wedding apparel and check for broken shoelaces, rumpled ties, and so on. Don't forget the buttonhole. You will also need to give your best man any monies required for church fees, if you have not already done so.

CHECKLIST: things the bridegroom needs to check on the wedding morning

1 Buttonhole
2 Has the best man got the ring
3 Substitute ring (just in case)
4 Luggage
5 Going-away clothes
6 Spare change
7 Taxi firm telephone number
8 Crib sheet

  9 Speech
10 Gifts
11 Going-away car keys

As a little light relief, you could reflect on the superstitions surrounding the bridegroom on his wedding day. These are fewer than the bride has to endure, but include:

* ☆ You must not see your bride in her wedding dress before you meet in church
* ☆ Dropping the ring before putting it on the bride's finger is bad luck
* ☆ If the bride helps the bridegroom in putting on the ring, she will rule the marriage
* ☆ All money paid out on this day must be handed over in odd sums
* ☆ The bridegroom must not turn back for anything after leaving for the church
* ☆ Whoever goes to sleep first on the marriage night will be the first to die. Mind you, the first to kneel at the service will also die first according to superstition, so the answer is clearly to make sure you do not do both, and one cancels the other out!
* ☆ You must carry your wife over the threshold when you enter your new home

THE WEDDING SERVICE

This section assumes that the marriage service is taking place in a Church of England church. For other denominations, see pages 71–73. However, in whatever faith the service is being held, the bridegroom will want to be at the church on time.

WHEN IS ON TIME?

On time means early – half an hour before the service is due to start. Allow for heavy traffic and tricky parking (it is likely the best man will be driving the car to the reception, and he will want to be able to get there quickly). This gives you a chance to check that the ushers are present and have been properly briefed, that there are sufficient service sheets (if you think they will run short, ask the ushers to give one to each couple, rather than each person).

Guests usually start to arrive from 25 minutes before the service. By then, or soon after, you should take your place in the front right pew, if possible walking down a side aisle. The bridegroom's role does not include greeting guests at the door. For some reason guests arriving at the service seem surprised if they see the bridegroom outside the church, and they will certainly start to worry if you are not inside it!

However, the best man may need to help the ushers out, and will want to meet the chief bridesmaid on her arrival (five minutes before the bride) to check all is well. He will also need to pay the fees due to the organist, choir, soloist, and bellringers – all in sealed envelopes which you should have handed to him previously.

This means the bridegroom can be left sitting at the front of the church, alone, nervous, for quite some time. Try not to fidget or turn round too much. Your family and friends will be seated in the pews behind you. Occasionally someone may lean over to say hello, and by all means have a quiet chat with them, but do not wander around the church exchanging greetings with people.

ARRIVAL OF THE BRIDE

On a pre-arranged signal (sometimes a flashing light, or maybe a wave from an usher) the organist will strike up the wedding march music to announce your bride's arrival. Everybody stands. Do not turn round at this moment, however tempted you are. Step forward to the chancel steps, facing the altar. Your best man will be a pace to your right and behind you. Now, with the procession well up the aisle, you can turn to give your bride a welcoming smile.

She will join you on your left, while her father stands behind and to the left of her. A bridesmaid will take her bouquet and if she is wearing one, lift back her veil. If there are no bridesmaids, the bride will hand her bouquet to her father, and you may lift back her veil for her. If this is the case, you must practise this several times the day before, to ensure you avoid catching her earrings or ruffling her hair. You should both turn and face the minister. At this point a hymn is usually sung, which gives everybody a chance to calm their nerves.

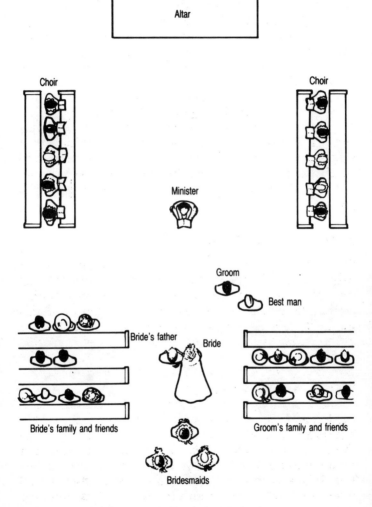

Positions as bride's procession approaches

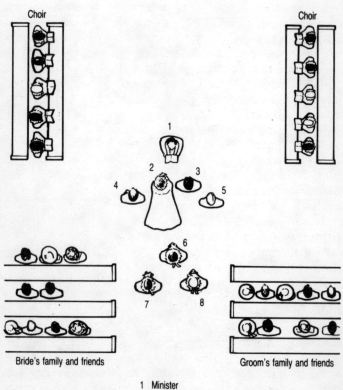

Bride's family and friends   Groom's family and friends

1 Minister
2 Bride
3 Groom
4 Bride's father
5 Best man
6 Chief bridesmaid
7 & 8 Bridesmaids

Positions for ceremony

Otherwise there may be a prayer and a reading from the Bible.

THE CEREMONY

The minister begins the ceremony, explaining the significance of marriage. He then asks if anyone present knows any reason why the couple cannot lawfully marry. Children and babies seem to sense the significance of the silence that follows, and often choose this point to yell or whimper. Actually if this happens it can break the tension, but do not let your concentration slip, for the vows come next.

First the minister asks you each in turn if you promise to love, comfort, honour and forsake all others (in the modern version), and protect the other 'as long as you both shall live', to which the answer is 'I will'. The minister then asks: 'Who gives this woman to be married to this man?' This is a signal for the bride's father to step forward, take his daughter's right hand and place it, palm down, in that of the minister.

You then take the bride's right hand, and exchange the vows that you take each other 'to have and to hold, from this day forward; for better, for worse, for richer, for poorer, in sickness and in health, to love and to cherish, till death us to part.'

You then turn to take the wedding ring(s) from the best man. Alternatively, he places the ring(s) on the minister's prayer book to be blessed. You then push the wedding ring gently down the third finger of her left hand (the bride should not be wearing her engagement ring at this stage). If you are exchanging rings, the bride will then put your ring in place. Try not to let your fingers shake! You then say:

I give you this ring
as a sign of our marriage.
With my body I honour you,

all that I am I give to you,
and all that I have I share with you,
within the love of God,
Father, Son and Holy Spirit.

You may be repeating the words of the minister, perhaps reading from a card hung from his book, or be reciting the words from memory. Whatever it is, remember you are facing forwards, with the congregation behind you. Speak as loudly as you can without feeling ridiculous. That way everyone will hear your words, and will be impressed at your confidence and commitment.

The bride responds with a similar promise, and the minister pronounces you man and wife, often then making a short address to the congregation.

SIGNING THE REGISTER

At the end of the service, the wedding party – bride and bridegroom, both sets of parents, best man and chief bridesmaid (who usually act as the witnesses) – join the minister in the vestry to sign the register. The bride signs first, using her maiden name, possibly for the last time. Photographs are often taken of the signing.

From now on, everything is much more relaxed, but the party should not linger too long in the vestry as any wedding due to take place shortly after would be delayed. You may need to wait for the ink on the marriage certificate to dry. The best man, or one of the mothers who is carrying a handbag, can take it away.

A signal should be given to the organist to commence the bridal march. You then lead the way from the vestry, with your new wife on your left arm. Behind you will be any small bridesmaids, the chief bridesmaid with the best man, the bride's mother with the bridegroom's father, the bridegroom's mother with the bride's father,

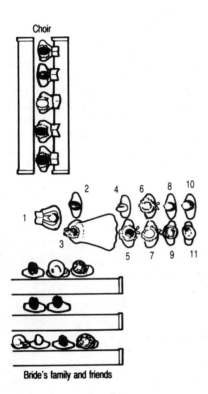
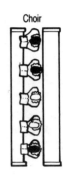
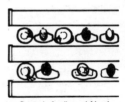

Altar

Choir

Choir

Bride's family and friends

Groom's family and friends

1	Minister	6 & 7	Bridesmaids
2	Bridegroom	8	Groom's father
3	Bride	9	Bride's mother
4	Best man	10	Bride's father
5	Chief bridesmaid	11	Groom's mother

Order in procession to vestry

and the bridesmaids, often escorted by the ushers. Walk as slowly as you can. Your guests will enjoy seeing you as man and wife for the first time, and you will be able to exchange smiles (but no words) with them as you progress down the aisle. Photographs are often taken at this time, so moving slowly helps with this, too.

LEAVING THE CHURCH

Your photographer may wish you to pose for photographs in the church porch or some other attractive location. Try to keep this session as short as possible since behind you there are often guests crowded around the door eager to come out to greet you. More photographs are taken when you leave the porch and stand in a position around which various other people can join you. Your best man can do much to organize the groups requested by the photographer. There tends to be a lot of milling around by guests, while you seem to be stuck in one place as various people are brought up to stand next to you!

BEING PHOTOGRAPHED

There is a knack to being photographed. Get in a natural position and try to relax your body so that you feel comfortable. Change your position between photographs – you might put your arm round the best man's shoulders, or shake hands with your father-in-law. Resist any temptation to plunge your hands into your trouser pockets, and ask a bridesmaid or page boy to hold your hat and gloves. Try to look happy! When you smile, try to show your teeth, otherwise you may find you simply look terrified in the pictures!

If photographs are not convenient, or if you know there is a more attractive setting for them at the reception venue, you will leave the church area fairly soon. Be prepared for a shower of confetti as you approach the car (the best man should remind guests if the church has requested that no confetti be thrown).

LEAVING FOR THE RECEPTION

The wedding is over. You can enjoy a little time with your bride, confess how nervous you felt during the ceremony, tell her how wonderful she looks, or just relax together. Behind you, an excited convoy is bringing your guests to the reception. You should have briefed the best man and ushers to ensure all guests have transport. For now, forget all that, and don't worry about a thing. You need a break before the next stint of hard work: the reception.

OTHER DENOMINATIONS

ROMAN CATHOLIC

Roman Catholic marriage ceremonies are conducted either as part of a Mass (called a Nuptial Mass) or outside Mass (usually when one of the couple is not of that faith). In both cases, there are two kinds of Entrance Rites. In one, the bridegroom, best man and brides-maids await the bride at the church door. When she arrives the couple is greeted by the priest, who then leads the procession to the altar. In the other, the bridegroom and best man sit on the front right bench as at Church of England services. The rest of the ceremony is similar to that described above, although obviously the words and rituals are those of the Catholic faith.

UNITED REFORM CHURCH

During the service the congregation is asked to pray for the couple. The usual declaration that there is no legal impediment to the marriage are given, and the couple's right hands are joined. They then make their vows. The bridegroom places the ring on his bride's finger while saying that it is given in God's name as a symbol of all they will share. If rings are being exchanged, the bride makes a similar statement as she places his ring. The Marriage Blessing follows, leading into prayers and readings.

METHODIST

The Methodist marriage ceremony is very similar to that described above.

SOCIETY OF FRIENDS

Quaker weddings are simple, and solemn, very much in the style of the typical Society of Friends gathering at which it takes place. There is no leader, just a group of people sharing their act of worship. At some point of their own choosing the bridegroom and bride take one another's hands, rise to their feet, and the bridegroom says: 'Friends, I take this my friend [name] to be my wife, promising, through Divine assistance, to be unto her a loving and faithful husband so long as we both on earth shall live.' His bride makes a similar declaration, and the couple then sign the wedding certificate in front of the Registering Officer. Two witnesses also sign it – although often the whole gathering also add their names. Rings are generally exchanged after the marriage.

JEWISH

When Jewish people marry, they must by law give notice to a registrar, but the marriage itself can be solemnized in a synagogue or private house, with the Secretary of the synagogue taking down the necessary details. Jewish marriage ceremonies vary between different synagogues, but the following is based on a typical Jewish wedding.

The bridegroom should arrive first and sits in the Warden's box with his father, future father-in-law and best man (the latter usually being chosen from the bride's or his family). The rabbi asks the bridegroom to approve the appointment of two witnesses, and accept the terms of the marriage document (*ketubah*). When his bride is due to arrive, the bridegroom stands under a canopy (a reminder of when Israelites were forced to live in tents). The bride's father escorts her to the canopy and she stands on the bridegroom's right.

After a series of blessings, and sometimes a short address by the rabbi, the bridegroom says: 'Behold, thou art consecrated unto me by this ring, according to the law of Moses and Israel.' He then places the ring on his bride's right index finger, her acceptance signifying consent to the union. The marriage contract is then read, and the seven Blessings of Marriage follow. At the end of these, the couple sip wine from the same cup, symbolizing their union through the best and worst of times. The bridegroom then throws the glass to the ground to show the weakness of marriage without love.

Then comes the signing of the marriage contract, and the group leaves the synagogue. The bride and bridegroom spend a few minutes together in private to denote their new status as man and wife, then greet their guests at the reception.

REGISTRY OFFICE MARRIAGE CEREMONY

The documentation required for a civil marriage ceremony has already been detailed, see page 36. The ceremony itself is far less formal than those described in the rest of this chapter. Only two witnesses are required, although the bride and bridegroom usually join a small party of friends and family at the registry office about ten minutes before the ceremony.

The marriage official gives a short address to the couple, who declare there is no legal impediment to the marriage. They then join hands and speak the words of the legal contract of marriage and exchange rings. A few minutes after they walked in through the door, they watch the two witnesses add their signatures to their own, and exit as man and wife.

Dress can be very casual but usually suits and dresses which can be worn at many other functions are chosen. The reception can be as large as any held after a church wedding, or may be on a much smaller scale.

THE RECEPTION AND THE SPEECHES

Wedding receptions are very hard work for the happy couple – but very happy work, too. What could be better than celebrating your marriage with all your friends and relations? Your in-laws will have decided what kind of reception to hold: formal or informal, sit-down or buffet-style meal, whether to invite extra guests who could not be fitted in at the wedding ceremony, and so on.

THE RECEIVING LINE

You can be pretty sure your in-laws will have decided on a receiving line to greet the guests. This may seem over-formal, but it does ensure that you have some contact with every person who comes to your wedding, and they will value it. The usual order of the receiving line is: bride's mother and father; bridegroom's mother and father; bride and groom, although sometimes the happy couple stand in the middle.

Inevitably a queue will form as guests wait to greet their hosts and enter the reception. If possible, it is a good idea for them to be served with drinks while they wait. As people pass up the line you will hear them

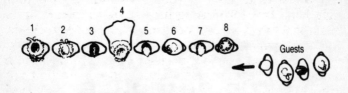

1 & 2 Bridesmaids
3 Groom
4 Bride
5 Groom's father
6 Groom's mother
7 Bride's father
8 Bride's mother

Typical receiving line

being greeted and/or introduced. Keep an ear out for this as it will help you to identify unfamiliar faces. The men will shake you by the hand, as will some of the women who do not know you, while the others may well offer their cheek for a polite kiss. To avoid nose-jarring collisions, follow the rule that it is always the left cheek which is offered by both of you.

Standing exchanging greetings with perhaps upwards of a hundred people, some of whom you have never met, is tiring. Even if your hand is sore from shaking hands, and your mouth aches from smiling, keep going and stay cheerful – no one cares for a gloomy bridegroom.

There is also nothing worse than one who has drunk too much. You may have been offered a drink (which you will have to hold in your left hand to leave your right hand free for shaking hands); by all means sip it, but make sure you do not drink it too quickly. Firstly, you will be mingling with your guests and need to keep your wits about you – especially if you are under the unforgiving eye of a video camera! Secondly, you are later to make a speech which must be clear and coherent. Finally, you may be driving yourself and your bride away from the reception. For these excellent reasons, the bridegroom should abstain from more than a couple of glasses of wine at the reception. Keep your glass topped up with mineral water for the toasts.

Find something personal to say to as many guests as you can. If you remember what their wedding gift was (your bride may be able to prompt you on a few) then a specific 'thank you' for it will please them greatly. Perhaps you know a particular couple has travelled a long way, or you have heard their names many times but not met them until now. There is usually something personal you can say if you work at it! Listen out for clues from what they say to other people in the receiving line, too.

Try not to enter into long conversations, even with friends of many years – tell them you will seek them out later on. Queuing for the receiving line can be rather wearing for the guests, especially if they are waiting in the open air or in a draughty entrance hall.

As the line of guests peters out, wait for the bride's father's lead in breaking out of the line. If there are still some formal photographs to be taken, now is the time, while guests socialize over their drinks, or take their seats for the meal. In the latter case, you should aim to join them as quickly as possible, as conversation and patience can flag while people wait for the top table to be occupied.

If the meal is a more informal buffet style with no top table, they could start to eat – the best man or master of ceremonies should take the lead here, either by example or by making an announcement. The announcement may include the saying of Grace, which is optional but should certainly be said if a minister or priest is present. You should of course be there for this, but can then slip away for more photographs.

TOP TABLE

If there is a top table a number of seating suggestions are shown opposite. The top table is occupied by the bride and bridegroom in the centre, both sets of parents on either side of them, best man and chief bridesmaid, possibly the other bridesmaids, depending on their age and the space available, and perhaps the chief usher. Obviously this will have been planned well in advance and there should be table cards to show people where to sit. Those sitting at the top table are invariably served first, or invited to go to the buffet first to be served if that is the style of the meal.

INFORMAL BUFFET

If the catering is buffet-style with no seating (and hence no top table) you will be free to mingle with your guests throughout the meal. Whether you go round the room separately or as a couple is a matter of personal choice. Many guests will enjoy seeing you together, but you will be able to get round to chat to more people if you split up. Perhaps the best solution is to split up initially, for you will inevitably meet up as you circulate. You can always send a message for your bride to join you if necessary!

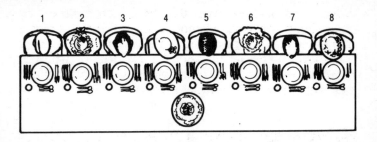

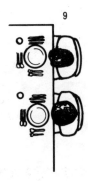

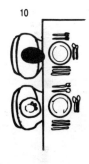

1 Best man
2 Chief bridesmaid
3 Groom's father
4 Bride's mother
5 Bridegroom
6 Bride
7 Bride's father
8 Groom's mother
9 Bride's family
10 Groom's family

Top table plan

One thing you must not do is settle down with your cronies in a corner: it is your duty to circulate as much as possible, and guests will think it very rude if you are not seen to be doing this. Equally, your friends are your ambassadors for the day, and it would be unforgivable if they were rude or unruly.

One problem for the bride and bridegroom at an informal buffet is that they are so busy circulating that they do not get a chance to eat! A solution is to have a plate with a selection of foods prepared and left in the room where you will change. That way you can be sure your stomach will not be rumbling as you make your exit from the reception.

THE SPEECHES

Now come the few minutes which three people have probably been dreading all day: the speeches. Comprehensive advice on planning and making a speech is given on pages 86–90. If you read this, and ask other people who have made speeches to give you some tips, you should be all right.

First to speak is the bride's father, or his representative, for he may invite an old family friend or relation to speak in his place. The speech will end with a toast to the bride and bridegroom, followed by a burst of applause.

Now it is your turn. Stay calm, give your speech as you have planned and rehearsed it, and speak as slowly as you can, as nerves give speakers a tendency to gabble. Your speech ends with a toast to the bridesmaids. If your bride wishes to say a few words as well, she should do so before this toast, which can then be proposed by both of you together.

The best man's speech is nominally on behalf of the

bridesmaids. It is bound to include some jokes at your expense. Even if you find some of these hard to take, keep smiling and do not show your annoyance – if people feel the best man has gone too far, they will feel sympathetic towards you anyway.

The speeches over, you can breathe a deep sigh of relief before cutting the cake.

CUTTING THE CAKE

The bride and bridegroom traditionally make the first cut of the cake together, after which the caterers whisk it away to slice it up frantically for serving to the guests.

The ritual is always a focus of attention, and invariably photographed. The danger is that the icing will be so hard you will not be able to cut through it with your uncomfortable joint grip on the knife. A bit of planning avoids the problem: ask the caterers, if the icing is hard, to make an incision through the icing while the speeches are being made. No-one will notice and you will be spared the embarrassment of a clumsy wrestling match with it in front of all the guests.

The bridegroom leads his bride to the cake so that they are both standing on one side of it. The point of the knife should be placed in the centre of the bottom tier, with the cutting edge towards the bride. The bridegroom then places his hand over his bride's, and together they push the handle gently down, drawing the blade slightly towards them. You are only making a token cut, and you may be asked to pause for photographs as you are slicing. Sometimes this ritual takes place before the speeches, giving the caterers more time to prepare portions for the guests to enjoy with their coffee. It is traditional to send pieces of cake to those who were unable to attend the wedding.

What happens next depends on what kind of reception is being held. If there is to be music and dancing, the bride and bridegroom lead the way to the dance area. They usually have one dance together, and are then joined by the rest of the top table, after which all the guests may dance if they wish. Some bridegrooms find this 'duet' more intimidating than making a speech. If you lack confidence about dancing in front of others, and do not want to invest in dance classes, you could at least practise with your bride in the weeks before the wedding. No-one is expecting a virtuoso display, but you will want to look and feel comfortable.

GOING AWAY

It is as well to plan the time of your departure. It helps the people who are running the event to have some idea of the timetable, and the going-away is important as it acts as a signal for other guests that they may now leave if they wish.

The bride and bridegroom retire to a room where their going-away clothes have been taken. The bride may ask her chief bridesmaid to help her out of her wedding dress. Otherwise she will probably ask you, so it is best to help her before you start to change too. If you wore morning dress for the wedding, you will probably now change into a suit. If the wedding was less formal and you are already wearing a suit, you should still change into something more casual.

When you are both ready, make a final check that you have everything you need for the rest of the evening and, if you are going straight to your honeymoon destination, that you have all necessary documents and luggage, or that they have been packed in the car.

You are not expected to continue socializing once you have changed into your going-away outfits. Of course you may pause for a quick chat with anyone you missed while circulating, but you should really be heading for your transport now. Some couples have left their reception by hot air balloon, helicopter, speed-boat, and even on bicycles, but chances are you will be leaving by car, either driving yourselves or in a taxi.

If your departure is by private car, it is very likely that the younger guests will have spent an enjoyable half hour decorating it with streamers, confetti, balloons, and anything else that could be attached to the car. If there is shaving foam sprayed on the windscreen, use the wipers to remove it before setting off – otherwise you risk driving over a guest's foot and spoiling the day. Any other adjustments can be left until you have driven a few hundred yards down the road and can safely pull in and remove anything that restricts your vision or could be dangerous. For example, balloons tied to radio aerials can be pulled by the drag of the car and break the aerial.

Make your departure as much fun as possible for the guests – toot the horn, flash the lights, wind down the windows and wave. Although celebrations often continue for many hours, this is an important symbolic moment in the day and it is fun to make it memorable.

If you are to make a long car journey, it may be worth organizing a decoy car in which to make your exit from the wedding. You can then drive to where your own car is parked and continue your journey. Make sure the person who loaned their car is aware of the purpose of the ruse (and that they will have to clear up the mess!)

and that there is some way of getting the keys back to them, unless they have a spare set with them.

Some couples hold a party in the evening after the reception. This gives them a chance to mix with their younger relations and friends without the inevitable restrictions imposed by a formal reception. Now you can let your hair down and really enjoy yourself with no responsibilities to worry about, except that if you both drink, you should take a taxi to where you are to spend the night.

CHECKLIST: at some stage after the wedding

1 Return hired wedding attire
2 Write thank you letters for gifts brought to the wedding
3 Distribute wedding cake
4 Distribute wedding pictures
5 Insure new possessions

MAKING A SPEECH

Weddings are a joyful celebration, but the prospect of making a speech to a large group of people can worry the bridegroom so much that he is unable to share in the pleasure of the day until his ordeal is over. This is sad because even a novice can, with careful planning and practice, make a perfectly good speech on these occasions. One point that you should always remember is that your audience is not hostile: it is composed of friends and relations who are here to wish you well.

PLANNING THE SPEECH

If you read a book of suggested speeches, use it only as a source of ideas, and do not simply recite one that you like. Sincerity is essential in the bridegroom's speech, and you can't get that out of a book. Jokes should be avoided. By all means make some funny comments, but do not launch into a series of witticisms that have no relation to the event, which is your wedding. Your speech is not the most important of the day, or expected to be rib-ticklingly funny (that's the best man's problem!) but it should reflect you as a person.

There are a number of things you must say:

1 Thank the previous speaker (usually the bride's father) who has proposed a toast to your and your bride's health.

2 Thank the bride's parents for organizing the wedding and for hosting the reception.
3 Thank other major contributors to the wedding (perhaps a friend decorated the cake, or an aunt produced the flower displays in the church).
4 Thank everybody for their gifts.

There may be other thanks you wish to add to this list of essentials. Thanking your own parents for their help over the last few weeks would be a nice gesture, as would a special mention of anyone who has travelled a long way or made a particular effort to come to the wedding.

You should aim to speak for 3–4 minutes. You will have to speak more slowly than you would in normal conversation so that you are easily heard and under-stood, which means the total number of words should be between 350 and 500.

PROMPT NOTES

Some bridegrooms write their whole speech on to cards, word for word. This can be a big help but the danger is that if you once lose your place, you could become panic-stricken and tail off rather embarrass-ingly. A better way is to write down reminders of what to say – a key phrase, the name of someone you would like to thank – in the right order. Your card might read something like this:

1 THANKS TO RICHARD FOR HIS KIND WORDS
2 WONDERFUL DAY
3 CHURCH LOOKED LOVELY – THAN YOU JEAN
4 MARVELLOUS RECEPTION – THANK YOU BARBARA AND RICHARD
5 NONE OF THIS POSSIBLE WITHOUT MY PARENTS

6 WHEN I FIRST MET MY NEW WIFE...
7 HOW DELIGHTED I WAS WHEN SHE ACCEPTED MY PROPOSAL
8 HOW BEAUTIFUL SHE LOOKS TODAY
9 HOW HELPFUL THE BEST MAN AND BRIDESMAIDS HAVE BEEN
10 TOAST TO THE BRIDESMAIDS

REHEARSING

Try reading the speech to yourself. Does it sound natural? Does it sound like you talking? Now read it out loud – you may feel pretty stupid doing this, but it is very helpful. You will find you have to pause for breath more now you are speaking out loud. If you have a tape recorder, put the microphone across the room and make your speech. Listen to the playback and ask yourself if all the words can be heard clearly and whether you spoke too fast. When you actually make the speech at the wedding you will find you speak a lot faster through nervousness, so work against this now by deliberately slowing down. A close friend listening to your speech might have some useful observations to make, too.

You should be quite familiar with your speech by now and be able to reel off whole sections word for word. Again, this will make you speed up, so slow down deliberately. Now deliver your speech standing in front of a mirror. Are you making any distracting gestures or movements – scratching your face, putting your hands in your pockets? The latter is fine, because it makes you look relaxed, so long as you don't keep pulling them out to make explanatory gestures.

GIVING YOUR SPEECH

When you are making your speech, try to pick out people in your audience to look at for a few seconds, then move on to another face. They do not have to be people you recognize: the point is to avoid looking down, or over people's heads. Have a glass of water handy in case you get a tickle in your throat. Speak up, as if you were conversing with someone at the back of the room, but don't shout. If there is a microphone for you to use, hold it about twelve inches from your mouth, don't move it around too much, and hold your prompt cards in the other hand.

GIFT-GIVING DURING THE SPEECH

You will probably have bought a number of gifts for other people, including:

☆ Bride's parents
☆ Your parents
☆ Bridesmaids
☆ Best man
☆ Ushers
☆ Other major helpers

You may choose to present these gifts later on, or if you have chosen jewellery for the bridesmaids, the day before so that they could wear their gifts. However, you can distribute some or all of these gifts during your speech, with your bride or a bridesmaid handing them out as you deliver your personal thanks.

THE HONEYMOON AND AFTER

The honeymoon marks the start of your married life together. The significance of this was perhaps much greater in years gone by. Today, for many couples it provides an opportunity to enjoy a special holiday, perhaps to a far-flung destination, or maybe just of a longer duration than usual.

After all the excitement of the build-up to the wedding and the big day itself, it is not uncommon for newly weds to feel a slight sense of let-down after the ceremony. So much planning and energy went into it, and now it is over. It can also feel very odd to have left behind all your friends and relations having a great time together. Don't be afraid to voice such thoughts – marriage is all about sharing, and you can help each other get over these feelings. Relaxing together will help, too, and will provide the best foundation for your new relationship.

MAKING A WILL

It is commonly assumed that when one of you dies, your estate passes directly to your spouse. This is not always the case. There are limits prescribed on how much can be automatically transferred in the absence of a will, and

the legal aspects of death are made far more complicated if there is no will. There are plenty of books giving
advice on how to make a will, or you could ask a local
solicitor to explain what you have to do.

INSURANCE

If you already have a life assurance policy, you will
probably wish to make your wife its beneficiary. If you
do not have one, now is a good time to consider taking
one out as it would help to provide for her if you died.

If you have moved into new home, make sure you
take out a policy to cover its contents – including all the
wedding gifts. Even if you are now sharing a house or
flat one of you owned, or were already living together,
you will need to add any expensive items you were
given to the contents policy.

STARTING A FAMILY

Even if you are not planning to have children at all, or
not for many years, once you are married people tend
to assume it is on the cards. Either or both your sets of
parents may be very keen for this to happen, especially
if they are not already grandparents.

It is best to be prepared for questions and comments,
and the first step towards this is to agree with each other
on whether, and when, you would like to have children.
Modern contraceptive methods allow us a choice in this
matter which was more difficult for previous generations to make. You may have talked this through during
your engagement, but even if you did, your or your
wife's thoughts might have changed. Allow a lot of time
for your discussions – one exchange of views will not be
sufficient to map out the pattern of the early years of
marriage.

MAKING MARRIAGE WORK

There is a lot of rubbish written and said about how to make marriage work. Phrases like 'Love is never having to say you're sorry' give a misleading idea that a loving bond is all you need to see you through life's challenges. It isn't. You have to work at marriage in the same way as you work at a job: make allowances, communicate your feelings, and think about your partner's needs as well as your own. About a third of today's marriages end in divorce, which is rarely amicable. If you show consideration to each other, and try to understand and work with each other, you might be able to avoid being part of that unhappy statistic.

If you do, you will have many wedding anniversaries to celebrate. Your wife will appreciate your remembering them without being prompted. If necessary, write the date into your diary at the start of each year! The anniversaries are listed below – you might have some trouble finding an appropriate gift for all of them!

Anniversary	*Wedding*	*Anniversary*	*Wedding*
First	Cotton	Fifteenth	Crystal
Second	Paper	Twentieth	China
Third	Leather	Twenty-fifth	Silver
Fourth	Books	Thirtieth	Pearl
Fifth	Wood	Thirty-fifth	Coral
Sixth	Sugar	Fortieth	Ruby
Seventh	Wool	Forty-fifth	Sapphire
Eighth	Bronze	Fiftieth	Golden
Ninth	Pottery	Fifty-fifth	Emerald
Tenth	Tin	Sixtieth	Diamond
Twelfth	Silk and linen	Seventy-fifth	Second diamond

INDEX

The Family Matters series:

A-Z of Childhood Illnesses 0 7063 6969 6
Anniversary Celebrations 0 7063 6636 0
Aromatherapy 0 7063 6959 9
Baby's First Year 0 7063 6778 2
Baby's Names 0 7063 6542 9
Baby's Names and Star Signs 0 7063 6801 0
Barbecue Tips 0 7063 6893 2
Card & Conjuring Tricks 0 7063 6811 8
Card Games 0 7063 6635 2
Card Games for One 0 7063 6747 2
Card Games for Two 0 7063 6907 6
Catering for a Wedding 0 7063 6953 X
Charades and Party Games 0 7063 6637 9
Children's Party Games 0 7063 6611 5
Christmas Planner 0 7063 6949 1
Common Ailments Cured Naturally 0 7063 6895 9
Does it Freeze? 0 7063 6960 2
Dreams and Their Meanings 0 7063 6802 9
Early Learning Games 0 7063 6771 5
First Time Father 0 7063 6952 1
Handwriting Secrets Revealed 0 7063 6841 X
How to be a Bridesmaid 0 7063 7003 1
How to be the Best Man 0 7063 6748 0
Microwave Tips & Timings 0 7063 6812 6
Modern Etiquette 0 7063 6641 7
Naming Baby 0 7063 5854 6
Palmistry 0 7063 6894 0
Preparing for Baby 0 7063 6883 5
Pressure Cooker Tips & Timings 0 7063 6908 4
Successful Children's Parties 0 7063 6843 6
Tracing Your Family Tree 0 7063 6947 5
Travel Games 0 7063 6643 3
Vegetarian Cooking Made Easy 0 7063 6941 6
Wedding Etiquette 0 7063 6868 1
Wedding Planner, The 0 7063 6867 3
Wedding Speeches and Toasts 0 7063 6642 5